MEET SUSIE & JOHNNY GRILLED CHEESE

CLUB

WRITTEN BY :
ERIN DULLAGHAN JONES

ILLUSTRATED BY :
PATITTOO ON FIVERR

D1155109

This book is dedicated to my sweet children, Amelia, Emerson, and Cambell. Celebrating all the special nights we spent imagining the adventures of Susie & Johnny Grilled Cheese. All the while snuggling, laughing, and just enjoying the moment.

This is a story about Susie & Johnny Grilled Cheese. They are the best of friends. They meet at the bus stop every morning and always are excited to see each other.

They talk about everything, including their favorite subjects at school and subjects they dislike. Then they immediately start planning for their after-school fun, which always includes a new adventure.

SUSIE

Meet Susie! She's kind, caring, and smart. She loves to act and play soccer with her BFF, Johnny. Susie has a little sister named Cecilia (Cece for short).

CECE

Her mom owns her own business, and Susie is constantly amazed by how her mom can hold her own business and then be the best mom in the world! Her Dad runs the Pink Palace Museum of Art & History.

Meet Johnny! He's silly, caring, and super playful. He loves playing outdoors, climbing trees, jumping rope, and jumping up and down on his trampoline. Johnny is the adventurous type.

He has twin sisters named Millie & Lillie, who are older and love to tease their little brother. His Mom is a teacher at his school, Tomato Soup Elementary. His Dad is an airplane pilot and flies worldwide, which Johnny thinks is rad!

DAD MOM

On their first day of school, both Susie & Johnny were super excited about the new year. They knew they were in the same class, which was so cool! As they entered the school building, they remembered the epic summer and sunshine fun they had.

As soon as they entered school, the first bell rang, and they quickly ran to their classroom to settle in for a new year of learning. Not only were Susie and Johnny best friends, but they were also outstanding students. Susie's favorite subject was world history, while Johnny loved math.

They were thrilled that they had the same schoolteacher for the first time; however, they realized that they couldn't say her name without a giggle... it was Ms. Furgosky. Furgosky! They couldn't tell anyone why they found it so funny, but they did. And sometimes, while in her classroom, they laughed so hard they got into innocent trouble.

Do you want to know why Susie and Johnny were so close? They truly felt like they were 'two peas in a pod' (if you do not know what that is saying means, ask your mom or dad) ever since they were babies. Both of their moms were regnant at the same time, and each mom delivered the babies on the same day in the same hospital. Their friendship was meant to be from the beginning.

While at school, they made other friends as most kids do, but they spoke a unique language that only the two understood. One day they headed to the school library, where they picked a famous Grilled Cheese to read about during the first month of school.

In addition, they were also assigned a project to a poster about these famous people. Johnny was to research Mr. Magilcutty, an Olympic athlete in swimming, and Susie was to discover more about Caroline Turner, the first female President of the United States.

Then as if things couldn't get any more exciting in the new school year, they were selected to build a set and develop characters for the school musical in which they would appear.

They picked their stage roles out of a hat, Johnny would be a pirate, and Susie would be a princess. They would be many other characters, such as a prince, mermaids, captains, and more. They were super pumped to start this project; however, the school bell rang, and it was time to grab their backpacks and head home.

Every day after school, the two youngsters would head straight to Johnny's kitchen, hungry and ready for their afternoon snacks. They ate all their favorite foods, with snacks like broccoli, brussels sprouts, cauliflower chips, and their ultimate favorite, pickle popsicles.

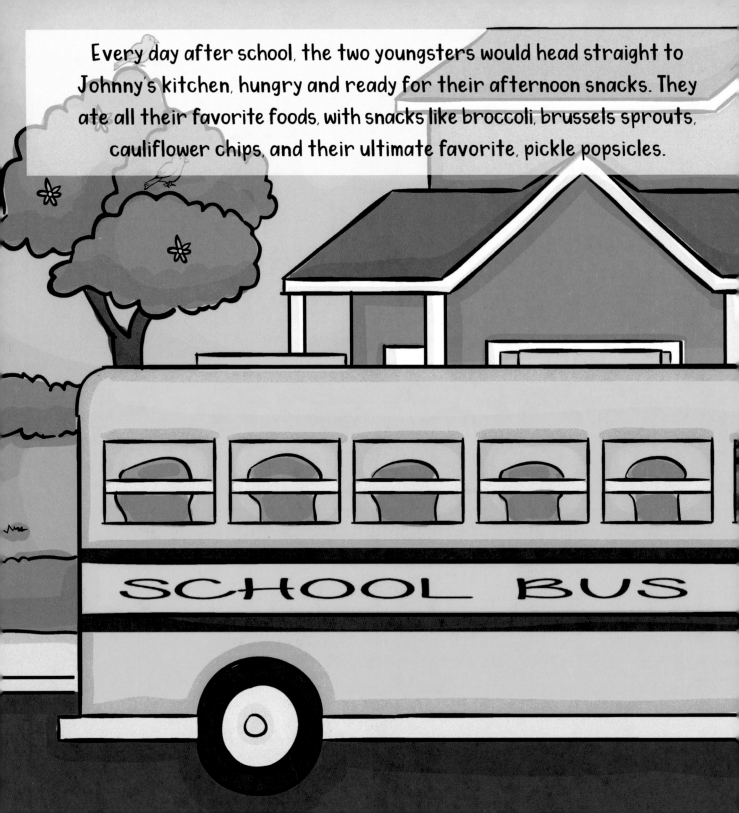

Next, they would zipline from Johnny's room, to their super secret treehouse, in which only they knew the code to get in, and upon arrival, every time, there was a secret clue for their adventure of the day! Then suddenly, their mystic vehicle makes itself known. Then their experience would begin.

They would be going to the Pink Palace Museum of History & Art this time. They started flying over the city until they arrived at the adventure location. Once there, they would enter through a secret door and ride their mystic car through history beginning in the 1800s.

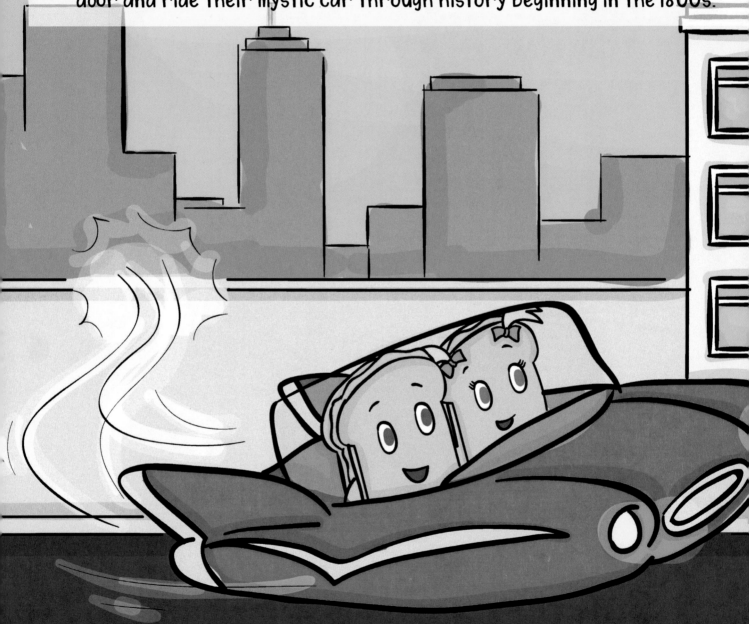

Susie and Johnny were thrilled with this adventure. They began to see living history scenes from the 1800s, 1900s, and 2000s. WOW!

Then could you imagine their surprise when they saw the two people they were researching for school? It was awesome because they took silly photos of the living statues and learned about their backgrounds. Soon after that, it was time to head back to the treehouse.

They had so much fun on their first adventure, and when they returned to the treehouse, another clue was waiting for them. They quickly opened it and saw that the next adventure would be an overnight expedition. While they tried to guess where it would be and what it would be, they were stumped because there was only a vague image on the clue.

They knew they would have to wait until it was time to find out where they would land. Where might they go on their next adventure?

Stay tuned for Susie & Johnny's next adventure coming soon!

About the Author

Along with her passion and commitment to the world of Public Relations and Marketing, Erin Dullaghan Jones has expanded her creative repertoire as an author and blogger with numerous projects over the past few years,which include the publication of her latest book, The Adventures of Susie & Johnny Grilled Cheese, an illustrated book for kids which was created with her three children.

Her career began immediately upon graduation from Western Kentucky University. She joined The Kentucky Derby Festival as the Director of Publicity and Communications Manager, Kentucky's, and the nation's largest festival hosting over 70 events each year. During her time at the festival, she also worked as a Broadcast Coordinator and Press Officer of the ESPN X Games; she coordinated media appearances for staff and participating athletes when the medium of alternative sports was emerging, then exploded into mainstream culture.

Whole Foods Market then enlisted Erin as their Louisville Regional Marketing Specialist, where she planned, supervised, and executed all public relations/media relations, special events, and promotions. Next up, she was the Director of Sales at Metromojo, LLC. Her supervision of sales process optimization, lead generation, qualification, contracting, and advertising performance was a considerable time when web organizations were in their infancy.

Erin founded in Mode Marketing in 2010, where her in-depth knowledge of the ever-evolving marketing world is distinguished. Her strategic expertise in Communications – Public Relations, Marketing, Crisis Communication, Social media strategy, and Event marketing – enhances the awareness of her diverse client base, which encompasses everything from philanthropy to consumer goods. Erin is also an accomplished speaker and trainer and has an impressive resume of public speaking engagements at keynote marketing-related events throughout the country.

Made in the USA
Monee, IL
28 February 2023

28790243R00033